WALKING WITH BARBARA:

30 Emails from God

By Barbara Hemphill

Blessings,
Barbara

ADVANCE PRAISE FOR WALKING WITH BARBARA

God speaks to us almost daily through Barbara. I have read these 30 emails twice. They are too precious to unread. Barbara is one of the igniting forces that have made us be what we are physically and spiritually.

Leivon Canary Kom
Shepherd's House Ministry, North East India

Walking with Barbara is phenomenal. She will make you smile and laugh as you feel her love through every email. It will give you a sense of peace as you read each email. Barbara changed my life the day I was on the treadmill and saw her on Good Morning America – National clean off your desk day. She inspired me that day to clean off my desk. Walking with Barbara: 30 emails from God is both inspiring and motivational. I thank God every day for Barbara Hemphill.

Pat Bender, President
Bayley & Bender

You will devour this book all at once and then will reread it to juice its truth, wisdom, and inspiration for your life and business.

Pooja Chilukuri, Nutrition and Health
Author, Nutritional Therapy Practitioner, Health Coach

Encouraging, supportive, and loving Barbara pours into you, builds you up, and helps you be the very best that you are capable of being.

Boris Wiggins
Founder of iEnCourageDaily

Now more than ever, we need guidance and faith. We live in "interesting times" and they seem to be getting more interesting by the day. I have been inspired by Barbara's passion for life and enjoyed reading this book from cover to cover. I now go back and read a page here and there when I need more inspiration. Barbara's faith and her sincere desire for you to accomplish your work and enjoy your life is fully appreciated as she shares both throughout the book.

Jeff Borschowa
Pharos Business Services Inc

Barbara Hemphill is a woman deeply guided by her faith, spirit, and purpose. Her life's meaning stems from her belief in a higher purpose for life and her strong connection with God. She shares in this book her deep convictions and stories and blessings in a manner that gently encourages us to do the same within ourselves, within whatever beliefs we each hold. It is a book of conversations that one can savor, return to, and feel nourished. We are all the better for Barbara's being in our lives and offering her wisdom.

Louise Wannier
Creative Entrepreneur, Artist. Author

I have the privilege of calling Barbara Hemphill a friend. Her heart and desire to love others are just as real as her friendship. Barbara walks out her faith every day through the relationships and opportunities she is engaged in. These 30 emails demonstrate that truth, and what we can learn from them will make us better together.

Dr. Boomer Brown, Ph.D., CEO
Doing Good at Work, Inc.

Barbara's writing illustrates that whether you live in a mansion or on main street in a small town, whether you are a business person or retired, we all share similar problems, and we all need someone who understands and cares.

Rosalie Scholl
Seamstress

What a joy it has been to watch this multi-talented author grow up! It was my gift to have her as a piano student from childhood through high school. She continues to bless audiences with her musical talent. She is a gift to me and all who are blessed to know her. I'm confident this latest book will bring everyone who reads it encouragement and hope.

Mildred Appleoff Marsh
Music Educator

Over the last 20 years, I've "walked" with Barbara in person, on the phone, online, and through her emails and books. Each time I come away with a deep appreciation for her gift of bringing a spiritual dimension to work and business. Now through this book, readers can experience the same insights that have inspired me and so many others."

Terri Lonier, PhD, Executive Advisor on Innovation
Founder, Authority By Design

Walking With Barbara is just that - an opportunity to hear and learn from one of the most hopeful and encouraging voices I know. Barbara showed up in my life at a critical point when clutter was winning and preventing my voice from being heard. Her words then, just like her words in this book, inspire me to go from good to best, to accomplish my work and enjoy my life. If you need words of encouragement, look no further. Hope is in your hands.

Helen Moses
Owner of Speak Up Communications and Author of Voice Unleashed: Speaking Up with Faith and Courage

I have known Barbara for over 20 years. She has been a role model for me and lives her life the way I desire to - walking with God. Her new book "Walking with Barbara" is a must read! The advice she gives and the stories she tells are priceless!

Elizabeth Hagen
Elizabeth Hagen Enterprises

Through her businesses, writing, speaking, and philanthropic efforts, Barbara inspires so many people. This book is no exception. Her heartfelt, spontaneous words draw you in, and you can feel the passion behind every message. You've come to the right place, whether you seek a snapshot of Barbara's wisdom or a delightful, faith-filled journey.

Kathy Muzik
New Path Productivity, LLC

Barbara is more than a kind person. She is in tune with her God-given purpose. That brings me hope.

Juliana Kathman
Organized by Juliana, LLC

Walking with Barbara is full of memorable stories that illustrate life-changing principles for organizing and decluttering. Many of her emails include practical concepts - which I love - but others include thought-provoking spiritual concepts, such as when she connected clutter to the Garden of Eden.

Liz Fackelman
Davidson Organizing, LLC

Barbara has been a great friend and mentor and I am honored to be part of her Productive Environment Program. I enjoyed reading her daily emails and am excited that they will now be available in book form.

Caren Osborne
Caren's Organizing Solutions, LLC

"Walking with Barbara" is an easy and enjoyable read. It is amazing to me that Barbara started each day with no strategy or plan, other than to simply write what was on her mind/heart/spirit for 30 days. There was no intention of turning those thoughts into a book, and yet there is such a beautiful flow through the entire book that you just know this was divinely inspired, and meant to be shared with the world.

Monica Young
MY Productive Biz

I am truly honored to be mentioned in Barbara's newest book "Walking with Barbara: 30 Emails from God", which started out as a simple (but not easy) email-writing project. I am forever grateful to have a front row seat to Barbara's adventures. I encourage you to read this book as if you're on an adventure with Barbara too. Buckle up and enjoy the journey!

Andrea Anderson, CEO
Productive Environment Institute

Walking with Barbara is a trove of treasures. It's filled with an abundance of practical advice and poignant stories that had me poring through the pages soaking up the amazing tidbits. But beyond the advice, Barbara offers another gift to her readers. It's the motivation she sparks in all of us to live our most authentic lives. No matter what age we are, Barbara leads the way in showing how to continuously show up for life with all its miraculous twists and turns. Her authenticity, vulnerability and commitment to her faith are stunning.

Dorena Kohrs
Space Doula

One of the best things that ever happened to me was meeting and watching Barbara Hemphill in the earliest years of my business. Barbara has always been a beacon of light, creativity, wisdom, insight and brilliance--a shining role model of what providing quality, grace and value in business looks like. Whether teaching organizing and time management, helping clients shape and pursue their goals, speaking, writing or coaching, there isn't a thing Barbara does that isn't effective and spot on to the needs of clients and audiences. I am lucky to have been mentored by Barbara, and consider her a friend, and role model for everything I do.

Julie Morgenstern
Founder & CEO, Julie Morgenstern

She's done it again! Barbara is a beacon of light and hope. She works tirelessly to offer services and programs that improve people's lives, wellbeing, and spread the glory of God. Her words, actions, and work align in uplifting all who cross her path, and this book is no different. Sit back and enjoy her golden nuggets of reflection and wisdom gleaned from years of experience and divine guidance.

Carolyn Byrd
Coach, Speaker, Author, and Founder of Cary Integrative Health

To know Barbara, is to love Barbara! You will love this book filled with encouragement and peace. Guaranteed to bless all who read it!

Ann Cueva
Custom Organizing, Inc.

I've known Barbara for about 25 years. Barbara is the real deal. She has been my mentor, my fellow organizer, my Bible study buddy and my dear friend. She has never wavered from her authentic spiritual beliefs that all personal experiences and relationships have power to help us grow and make life rewarding. That rich life experience and Barbara's organizing skills are offered up right here in this little gem of a book. Don't waste a minute of time. Read it!

Anne Sedler
Retired Certified Productive Environment Specialist

Barbara signed up for my 21 Day Prophetic Whiteboard Session. On day one, her key objective was to care for the poor and give a certain amount of money every month. I was impressed by her love and passion for the poor. As time went by, I learned that she had been carrying this desire for most of her life, and today this book is a testament to her mission and perseverance. Well done, friend of God. See you at the top!

Melvin Pillay, President
Pillay International

WALKING
WITH
Barbara

30 EMAILS
FROM GOD

BY BARBARA
HEMPHILL

Walking with Barbara: 30 Emails from God
2022© by Barbara Hemphill
All rights reserved. Published 2022.

Scripture quotations marked (NIV) are taken from THE HOLY BIBLE, NEW INTERNATIONAL VERSION ® NIV ® Copyright © 1973, 1978, 1984 by International Bible Society ® Used by permission. All rights reserved worldwide.

Scriptures marked (KJV) are taken from the KING JAMES VERSION (KJV): KING JAMES VERSION, public domain.

Cover Design: Spirit Media
Photo credit front cover: Brandi K Autry Photography & Design – Willow Spring NC
Editors: Kevin White

Printed in the United States of America
Spirit Media
www.spiritmedia.us
Spirit Media, and our logos are trademarks of Spirit Media
1249 Kildaire Farm Rd STE 112
Cary, NC 27511
(919) 629-9899

RELIGION / Christian Ministry / Missions
Paperback ISBN: 978-1-7377758-4-3
Hardback ISBN: 978-1-7377758-5-0
Audiobook ISBN: 978-1-7377758-6-7
eBook ISBN: 978-1-7377758-7-4
Library of Congress Control Number: 2022908342

SPIRIT MEDIA

Register This New Book

Benefits of Registering*

- FREE **replacements** of lost or damaged books
- FREE **audiobook**—Get to the Point by Kevin White
- FREE information about new titles and other **freebies**

www.spiritmedia.us/register
*See our website for requirements and limitations

To Jesus Christ, my Lord and Savior, who has guided me through these 75 years even when I didn't feel Him.

To my husband of 35 years who has "blocked and tackled so I could fly."

To Glenna Salsbury who role-modeled the impact of sharing Jesus in the workplace.

To Perry Marshall who offered the writing challenge that made this content possible.

To Andrea Anderson, Marj Gross, and Edz Buscano, without whom this book would not exist.

TABLE OF CONTENTS

FOREWORD

If you could take a walk with anyone who would it be?

Perhaps you'd choose someone famous, a loved one who passed years ago, or a Bible character?

I want to recommend you add Barbara Hemphill to your list.

Often, we glamorize famous people. Nothing wrong with fame. Yet, it's the ordinary people in our lives that make the greatest investments.

Barbara Hemphill has traveled the world and impacted thousands of people through her life and business. Everyone who knows her knows she is as down to earth as anyone.

Every time I've talked to Barbara, she has taught me something. She has invested in me. And she has done it unintentionally. It is just who Barbara is. And she has shared this gift with everyone she meets.

From grandpas to teachers, we've all had those people who made lasting impressions on our lives. They didn't schedule a life coaching session with us. They were just themselves. They were unaware of their investment. They weren't trying to accomplish anything. They were just themselves and it made us better.

That's Barbara Hemphill.

For instance, Barbara thought she had failed to reach her goal of writing a book for her 75th birthday. God used her friends and colleagues to encourage her to publish this book. Barbara saw simple emails. While God saw a book.

As you will see, each email is filled with practical wisdom, honest transparency, coaching, counseling, and inspiring stories. Barbara was just writing as unassuming Barbara. She had no agenda except to complete a writing assignment. She was just being Barbara. Fortunately, this book now allows some of this walk with Barbara to be "bottled up" and shared with people all around the world.

Perhaps Barbara can fill in for the grandmother, mentor, or coach you never had. Come take a walk with Barbara and hear God speak into your life through her emails from God. Your life will be all the richer.

Kevin White
Founder/Executive Director, Global Hope India
CEO, Spirit Media

INTRODUCTION

At the beginning of 2021, I shared with my business partner and CEO of Productive Environment Institute (PEI), Andrea Anderson, that I wanted to write a book to celebrate my 75th birthday. I had pages of notes about the possibilities of what I could write, and I discussed numerous ideas with a publisher with whom I had worked. Then in August, I had a horseback riding accident and broke my collarbone. As a result, it was challenging to use my computer, and the pain slowed my creativity.

The PEI team, the "Faithful Five," meets virtually every Monday morning for prayer. The Monday before my birthday, Andrea announced that they wanted to hold a special meeting on December 30 to celebrate my birthday, and of course, I agreed!

Andrea began the meeting by saying, "Barbara, we knew you wanted to write a book for your 75th birthday, and we want to show you that you did! Edz Buscano coordinated taking the content you wrote in the 30-Day Email challenge given to you by Perry Marshall and created what you see here." Much to my astonishment, she brought up a beautifully designed and illustrated e-book which Spirit Media turned into the book you are holding.

I've always loved the story in Exodus where God told Moses to stand on the top of the hill with the staff of God in his hand. As Moses obeyed, Israel prevailed in the battle against Amalek, but whenever he lowered his hand, Amalek prevailed. "But Moses' hands grew weary...so Aaron and Hur held up his hands, one on one side, and the other on the other side. So, his hands were steady until the going down of the sun. And Joshua overwhelmed Amalek and his people with the sword."

One of the guiding principles of PEI is "Together We Are Better," and this book is the outcome of that truth. I shall forever be grateful, and I pray God's blessing on you as you read it.

EMAIL 1

TELL ME MORE

From: Barbara Hemphill
Subject: Tell Me More

First of all, I want to say "thank you" for signing up for this new project of publishing 30 emails in 30 days without writing them ahead of time. I'm honored by your interest and incredibly excited to see what happens! I decided to launch this adventure for three reasons:

1. I trust the business coaches, Perry Marshall and John Fancher, who recommended the idea and explained that the process would change the way my brain thinks.

2. For several months, I have been coaching with Judy Greenman in a course called Body Brain Freedom and have become acutely aware of the ability to change my life regardless of my age.

3. I love to use writing as a way to share ideas, and my mind is racing with anticipation. So here goes!

For several years I have begun each day in "The Doris Chair," named by my husband Alfred in honor of my mother, for whom we purchased it, in anticipation of her living with us a few months of the year. Unfortunately, she died before that happened, and I turned that room into the place I begin my day listening for what God would like me to hear.

My grandfather was a very devout Christian and repeatedly said, "God told me..." As a child going to a one-room school where schoolmates bullied me and I often felt alone and lost, I begged God to speak to me, as well. But all I heard was silence. At one point, Granddad said, "If you don't hear from God, it's because you have skeletons in your closet." I have often joked, "I started an organizing business clearing the clutter from closets in an attempt to hear from God."

I have since learned that God speaks to me in many ways, none of them in an audible voice, but now I crave hearing more. I titled this post "Tell Me More" because I am confident that we could solve many of the problems in our lives and our world if we used that phrase more often.

I think it was Mark Twain who said, "The older I get, the more I don't know." I've learned that saying "Tell me more," whether to God, to a family member, or a colleague, and then genuinely listening can be a profound source of valuable information and greater peace.

So, here's my thought for today: The next time someone says something you don't understand or that makes you angry or upset, try saying, "Tell me more," and see what happens. I welcome your comments.

Blessings,

Barbara

Barbara Hemphill, Founder
Productive Environment Institute
Helping Professionals Accomplish Their Work and Enjoy Their Lives!

THE PIANOS IN MY LIFE

From: Barbara Hemphill
Subject: The Pianos in My Life

"Life is like a piano; the white keys represent happiness and the black show sadness. But as you go through life's journey, remember that the black keys also create music." - author unknown.

Recently, I read an editorial in The Washington Post by John Ficarra entitled "Farewell, my beloved old Baldwin Piano." He told the life story of the piano he purchased at great sacrifice at a young age being hauled away with the horrible thought it might end up smashed into firewood.

Reading it reminded me of the significance and blessing of pianos in my life.

My life began with a piano. My mother's parents lived in Kansas and managed what was then called "The County Poor Farm," where people who had no home or family went to live. Despite the fact money was scarce, they somehow scraped together $800 to purchase a piano for my mother, which she took to the farm in Nebraska where she and Daddy lived throughout their marriage.

At a very young age, about five, I think, my parents sacrificed to give me piano lessons. I recall hearing Mom saying, "I could tell the kind of day you had at school by the music you were playing when I came home from work." My mother had a beautiful voice, and I soon began accompanying her solos in our old country church. During my high school days, I accompanied numerous vocal groups. A highlight of my life was accompanying an opera singer, whose name I can't remember, when she came to my small town and sang a concert in the home (I thought it was a mansion!) of a resident.

In college, the piano was a cornerstone of my life. At one point, I accompanied 13 music ensembles. A highlight of my college experience was traveling to Europe with the college choir as an accompanist, and an experience surpassed only by my senior recital. At the end of the concert, Mom said, "You looked like you were having so much fun. I was more nervous than you were, having so much fun." She was right.

In 1971 I lived on the island of Grenada in the West Indies with my first husband, where I worked as a volunteer for Church World Service. It was a beautiful island, and while I have many happy memories and am grateful for the experience, my life there was challenging and sometimes frightening. I had a history of depression which deepened while I was there. At one point, I stopped driving the car because as I drove over the steep mountain roads, I began imagining how easy it would be to go off the mountainside, and no one would know it was intentional. Fortunately, I couldn't bring myself to do it because I knew how devastated my family would be and how God would feel about it.

One of my biggest blessings was an old upright piano left by the previous renter in our house. It was horribly out of tune, and we didn't have the money for a piano tuner, but in the piano bench I found a treasure. A piece of vocal music written by French composer Charles Gounod entitled "O Divine Redeemer." I had never heard the song before, but the words spoke to my heart. Often, I was crying too hard to sing, but I played the music and read the words as I played the piano—over and over again.

When we moved to India, there was no piano at first, but not long after we arrived, my grandmother (the one who had made sure my mother had a piano) died and left me $600. At that same time, I discovered that a German family was departing India and wanted to sell their beautiful hand-made 6 1/2 foot Pleyel piano. I began teaching piano to expatriate adults who found themselves in India because of their spouse's work and had time to pursue piano lessons. A highlight of my life in India was a goodwill music tour around the country as an accompanist to a soloist sponsored by USIA (United States Information Agency). Smiles on the faces of the audience canceled out the distress of playing out-of-tune pianos with many stuck keys.

As we prepared to leave India, I'll never forget the sight of the piano lumbering on an oxcart on its way to the ship to meet me in New York City. It arrived with a broken sounding board, but I was ecstatic to find a man to rebuild it.

When we moved from New York City to the Washington, DC, area and began looking for a place to live, it became a challenge to find a place we could afford with room for our three adopted Indian children—and my grand piano.

When my marriage ended, I moved into a small apartment. My piano and a small table with two chairs filled the living room.

I remarried and moved into our first home. My husband's best friend loves to recall the story of him and his three sons laboring to get that six-and-a-half-foot' grand piano into our living room.

When we moved to North Carolina 26 years ago, the piano came with us and became the centerpiece of our living room. One day I asked my assistant, Holly, to make an appointment to tune the piano. The piano-tuner refused, saying, "This piano belongs in a museum."

Through the grace of God and a saga too long to write today, a handmade Czechoslovakian piano made by the Petrof company sits in that space. I am thankful for it every day, and it continues to bring me joy in ways I can never express.

Blessings,

Barbara

Barbara Hemphill, Founder
Productive Environment Institute
Helping Professionals Accomplish Their Work and Enjoy Their Lives!

OUT OF SIGHT OUT OF MIND—NOT!

From: Barbara Hemphill
Subject: Out of Sight Out of Mind—NOT!

In the 40+ years I've been encouraging people to create filing systems, the most often repeated objection to putting papers in a file folder in a file cabinet is "out of sight out of mind." I understand.

Frequently, people who try to create a filing system ask the question, "Where should I FILE this?" That is the wrong question. The more helpful question is, "How can I FIND this?" There are so many ways you can file the same information: car, auto, vehicle. The problem is remembering what you called it when you want it again, and the chances that someone else looking for that information would think of the same answer is highly unlikely!

The solution is simple: a file index. A file index is to managing your physical documents what a chart of accounts is to managing your money.

One of the most rewarding outcomes of my career is our concept of creating a "Finding SYSTEM" instead of a "filing system." (Note: the acronym SYSTEM stands for Saving You Space Time Energy Money which is a most desirable outcome!)

Our approach to filing eliminates that nagging "out of sight out of mind" fear. It's far easier to look at a list of your files than to look through stacks of paper or boxes of paper. We create the list on your computer in a program you are already using regularly, or if you don't have one, we offer an option we find highly user-friendly.

Our method allows you to add as many keywords as you like for the same document. In addition, you can add reminders for when you want to access the information or what you want to do with it.

I advise our clients, "If there is something that you want to be able to retrieve easily, and it will fit in a file folder, with the Finding SYSTEM, you can be sure you will find it.

Clients often tell our Certified Productive Environment Specialists™ (CPES™), "Oh, that won't work for me." We ask them to "trust the process" and assure them that if they don't like the result, we can easily convert it to the traditional method to the piles on their desk!

If you'd like to explore whether a Finding SYSTEM would be a happy solution for you, go to www.ProductiveEnvironmentScore.com

Blessings,

Barbara

Barbara Hemphill, Founder
Productive Environment Institute
Helping Professionals Accomplish Their Work and Enjoy Their Lives!

EMAIL 4

WHAT ARE YOU HIDING?

From: Barbara Hemphill
Subject: What Are You Hiding?

Many years ago, a mother of five grown children hired me to help her organize her home. I don't remember her name, but I've never forgotten the look on her face when I held up a beautiful evening gown hidden in her closet. I asked, "How does this make you feel?" There was a pregnant pause and a tear in the corner of her eye as she replied, "Sad."

Out of that experience came the oft-repeated advice: "When something causes you to feel anything negative—depressed, guilty, fat—you can't afford to keep it."

In yesterday's post, I discussed the "out of sight out of mind" fear that plagues people when it comes to filing papers. Today I want to address another aspect of that concept. What about all the physical "stuff" we hide in our lives? We think it's hidden, but in my experience with thousands of clients, it isn't.

One client had an attic full of items left behind long ago by her grown children. We wrote a letter (remember when we used to do that?) to each of her children, giving them a time frame by which they needed to remove their items, or she would donate or toss them. I talked to her a few days after the attic was empty. She said, "You won't believe this, but I sleep better at night." The attic was above her master bedroom. While those items were "out of sight," they were not "out of mind."

Since Covid, we've had conversations with several businesses in the financial world that are legally required to keep documents for many years. In the paper world, that meant rows of filing cabinets and banker's boxes in storage—and often in the owner's basement or garage! While most firms have been paperless for several years, few have addressed the issue of how to handle what we euphemistically call "archives."

One of the positive outcomes of Covid is an increased recognition that as we often tolerate items in our lives which, while they may be out of sight, are not out of mind.

Why is it so difficult to "let go"? In my book, *Less Clutter More Life* (lesscluttermorelife.com), there is a list of the most common reasons:

- I don't have time.
- I have better things to do.
- It's too difficult.
- It never lasts.
- I didn't create it; I have no idea what's there.
- I'm easily distracted and go off on tangents.
- I get stuck in the memories of the past.
- It's too emotionally draining.
- I want to be responsible and respectful of what I've been given.
- I have to take care of other people and other things in my life first.
- It's hard to admit I have an issue.
- I'm afraid I might want it back.

What have you hidden? What prevents you from letting go? If you're not sure, but you want to, schedule a complimentary 30-minute Discovery Session with our team at:
www.ProductiveEnvironment.com

I'm passionate about helping you accomplish your work—AND enjoy your life!

Blessings,

Barbara

Barbara Hemphill, Founder
Productive Environment Institute
Helping Professionals Accomplish Their Work and Enjoy Their Lives!

MENTORING: SHARING YOUR GIFTS

From: Barbara Hemphill
Subject: Mentoring: Sharing Your Gifts

I love the suggestions I am getting from readers about topics—feel free to keep them coming!

Today, I will talk about a subject that has been and continues to be very important in my personal and professional life: mentoring. So many mentors have blessed me!

The word probably came into being in Homer's epic, *The Odyssey*. Odysseus was away from home fighting and journeying for 20 years. During that time, Telemachus, the son he left as a babe in arms, grew up under the supervision of Mentor, an old and trusted friend. When the goddess Athena decided it was time to complete the education of young Telemachus, she visited him disguised as Mentor. They set out together to learn about his father.

Today, we use the word *mentor* for anyone who is a positive, guiding influence in another (usually younger) person's life.

One reader asked three great questions:

1.   How do you get started?

2.   How do you discover your mentees?

3.   How do you approach them?

I've been participating in an intriguing program called "Body Brain Freedom," and one of the cornerstones of the work is the word "notice." I'm beginning to appreciate that all growth and change start by noticing, which certainly applies to mentoring.

You can get started as a mentor by noticing two things:

1.   What problem in the world do you see, about which you have knowledge and concern?

2.   Who are the kind of people for whom you have a big heart?

For example, I believe that God created every individual for a specific purpose. Unfortunately, many people are not aware of their purpose, or in some cases, know deep in their heart what it is, but aren't doing anything about it! That is a problem I have a passion for solving.

I have a big heart for people who are "stuck." They are intelligent and have valuable gifts, but they are not moving forward due to various circumstances, often from very early in their lives or from some current situation. Because of over four decades in the organizing and productivity industry, I often see that "stuckness" as physical, digital, emotional, or spiritual clutter.

That brings me to the second question, "How do I find them?" The answer: Going to or participating virtually in communities where "seekers" are—listening to conversations—asking questions. Utilize the phrase I discussed in my first email in this series: "Tell me more."

The third question of "How do you approach them?" can be answered with another of my favorite questions: "What WILL you do?" The biggest challenge for the productivity consultants we train is "What should I do to get clients?" to which we reply, "That's the wrong question!" and then ask them a question: "What WILL you do?" There are so many ways to connect with people—the solution is finding a way that most fits your style. I am a fan of making phone calls unannounced and saying, "Hi, this is Barbara Hemphill. Did I catch you at a bad time?" I'll often get an "I have a few minutes" response, giving me enough time to say what I want to say or schedule a more convenient time to talk. I have also made many meaningful connections with handwritten cards and physical letters.

If you do a Google search on "mentoring," you will find many resources, such as www.Mentoring.org

Happy mentoring!

Blessings,

Barbara

Barbara Hemphill, Founder
Productive Environment Institute
Helping Professionals Accomplish Their Work and Enjoy Their Lives!

WHO DO YOU ENCOURAGE?

From: Barbara Hemphill
Subject: Who Do You Encourage?

I don't know about you, but I need encouragement every day! A significant source for me is the Bible. One of my favorite verses is Joel

2:25 (NIV) in the Old Testament: *"I will repay you for the years the locusts have eaten..."*

For many years I was in a coaching program with Dan Sullivan, founder of The Strategic Coach®. Yesterday, I wrote about "mentors," and he has been a significant one for me. Dan spoke about how entrepreneurs continually operate in "The Gap." We quickly skip over what we have accomplished and jump to what we have failed to achieve. I'm still guilty of that sometimes, but I'm getting better, and that verse in Joel is one of the reasons. Whenever I feel sad or distressed about something, I intended to do but haven't, and now the opportunity has passed, or I'm fearful that I'm too old to make it happen, I take heart from this verse.

Here's one of my most vivid examples: My first marriage ended in divorce after 14 years. I was devastated. I admired my husband greatly. No one in my family had ever divorced. We had adopted three orphan children together. I was terrified.

When I was traveling with one of our consultants in Oregon, I purchased a plaque that hangs in my kitchen, which reads: "Marriages are not made in heaven. They come in kits, and you have to put them together." If I had been creating this, I would have added, "Over and over again!" Soon I will celebrate 35 years of marriage with Alfred!

My first husband is happily married to a wonderful woman, and our three adopted children are all fantastic adults.

My story of our marriage is a dramatic example of God restoring the years, but I could write volumes about how it happens every day in my life in small ways. Indeed, this admonition applies not only to entrepreneurs but to everyone!

Another of my mentors, Perry Marshall, encourages his students to spend at least 20 minutes each morning reading something written before the printing press. Why "before the printing press"? Because it is an indication of wisdom, and what better source of wisdom than Proverbs. Ironically, it has 31 chapters so that you can read one chapter a day each month! Proverbs 16:9 (KJV) reads: *"A man's heart deviseth his way; But the Lord directeth his steps..."*

Just last week, I made plans to travel to Arizona to discuss collaboration with the founder of a program I highly respect. The trip meant missing two other opportunities, but I decided to go, understanding that the company was paying my expenses. Then I learned that the owner did not intend to pay the travel costs, so we planned a Zoom meeting instead. As a result, we can still discuss collaboration, and I can participate in the other local activities.

When I hear someone expressing discouragement in our training program for productivity consultants, I often say, *Remember: It will all turn out in the end. Otherwise, it isn't the end yet.* (John Lennon said something similar, but I like this version better!)

During these challenging post-Covid days with so much uncertainty about what lies ahead for our world, our country, our communities, our families, our businesses, and ourselves, I challenge you to be a source of encouragement whenever you can. And when you fail, as we all do, take heart that God can restore our mistakes!

Blessings,

Barbara

Barbara Hemphill, Founder
Productive Environment Institute
Helping Professionals Accomplish Their Work and Enjoy Their Lives!

EMAIL 7

SEVEN BEDROCK PRINCIPLES OF PRODUCTIVE ENVIRONMENT INSTITUTE

From: Barbara Hemphill
Subject: Seven Bedrock Principles of Productive Environment Institute

When I began in the organizing industry over 40 years ago, I had no idea that I would end up with a team of Certified Productive Environment Specialists™ (CPESs) who have clients worldwide.

In this post-Covid world, it's an inspiring place to be, with many opportunities to help individuals and organizations accomplish their work and enjoy their lives. I feel very blessed.

The four words which have guided me since the beginning are: **Clutter is postponed decisions.®** Through the years, I've identified these seven bedrock principles to address that problem:

1. **Today's mail is tomorrow's pile.™**

    One of the biggest mistakes clients make is clearing up the mess without creating a system to prevent it from happening again—or at the very least, making it far easier to recover when it does, which it inevitably will.

2. **The Productive Environment Process™**

    I'll never forget the day sitting in a training session at Strategic Coach® when Dan Sullivan asked, "How do you do what you do?" "I have no idea," I replied, "I just do it!" Through the years, we have modified "what I do" to a five-step process you can use to solve any problem.

    a. State **your** vision.
    b. Identify **your** obstacles.
    c. Commit **your** resources.
    d. Design and execute **your** plan.
    e. Sustain **your** success.

Notice the common word: **"your"**!

After a speech in which I discussed the process, a woman excitedly came to the front of the room and said, "I can use that to work on my marriage!"

3. **The Art of Wastebasketry®**

Forty-plus years clearing clutter in homes and offices has confirmed the truth of the Pareto Principle (80/20 rule): Eighty percent of what we keep, we never use, and the more we keep, the less we use, either because we don't remember we have it, or we can't find it! To determine what you want to keep, ask this crucial question: "What's the worst thing that would happen if I got rid of this, and it turned out I was wrong?" If you can live with your answer, shred, recycle, or toss—and live happily ever after!

4. **The Cost Factor™**

Prospects are sometimes concerned about hiring us to help them out of fear that we will make them throw away everything. Here's our philosophy: "You can keep everything you want if you are willing to pay the price: time, space, money, and energy." Our job is to help you understand the cost to make an educated decision that will help you accomplish your work and enjoy your life.

5. **What a Difference a Few Hours Can Make!**

One of our clients was a company with 400 employees in the process of moving to a new location and going paperless. Each employee participated in a one-day event. We spent the morning clearing physical clutter, and the afternoon focused on digital clutter. The IT department measured the amount of space they were using. After three and one-half hours, we had deleted almost one-half of the digital files. One executive went from 24,000 to 4,000 emails in her inbox!

6. **File-Act-Toss!**

Often, we look at a pile of papers—or an overflowing email Inbox—and feel overwhelmed. The good news is that it's not nearly as complicated as you imagine. There are only three decisions you can make about any documents: File, Act, or Toss.

7. **The Power of SYSTEM (Saving You Space Time Energy Money)**

I learned early in my career that "Clutter is postponed decisions®." It was several years before a colleague made the statement, "It's not enough to make the decision. You have to have a way to implement it." A SYSTEM is a way to implement the decisions you make. Every time there is something you repeatedly do, you need a SYSTEM.

Blessings,

Barbara

Barbara Hemphill, Founder
Productive Environment Institute
Helping Professionals Accomplish Their Work and Enjoy Their Lives!

SPEAKING (PRAYING) IN PUBLIC: FEAR NOT!

From: Barbara Hemphill
Subject: Speaking (Praying) in Public: Fear Not!

Often, after a presentation or a Bible study that I have led, someone will comment, "I'm terrified to speak. I don't know how you do that." When I first began my organizing business in New York City in 1978 and needed to promote my services and had no money to buy advertising or hire someone to do it for me, speaking was my only option. I majored in music in college, which taught me performance skills, so I wasn't afraid of being in front of an audience, but the thought of promoting myself was terrifying. God sent me an answer in the form of a book by Dorothy Sarnoff, founder of Speech Dynamics, given to me by a client who was getting rid of her clutter! (Side note: I learned that many clients feel guilty getting rid of personally autographed books because they didn't want to be disrespectful. For that reason, I now autograph my books generically, so the recipient can comfortably pass it on to someone else!) Ironically, Dorothy Sarnoff was an opera singer, which touched my musical heart! She offered a four-step process to say to yourself before going before your audience:

- I'm glad I'm here.
- I'm glad you're here.
- I know what I know.
- I care about you.

Let's break it down:

1. **"I'm glad I'm here."**

   If you are not glad to be there, the question to ask yourself is, "Why did I agree to this?"—and think twice before you do it again! The only reason to speak in public is that you have something to say that you believe and feel will add value to the audience.

2. **"I'm glad you're here."**

   Think of speaking in public as an opportunity to be a positive influence on another person. As Trey Gowdy once said so eloquently, "People do not listen in groups; they listen as individuals." That means you do not need to be afraid of the crowd.

3. **"I know what I know."**

You are not standing in front of an audience because you have a solution to all the attendees' problems. You are there because there is something you know that will benefit them. If someone asks a question for which you have no answer, it's perfectly appropriate to say, "I don't know—that's out of my wheelhouse," or "That's a great question, and I'd love to find out. Give me your contact info, and I'll share with you what I learned!"

4. **"I care about you."**

If you don't care about your audience, it's not the right audience for you. I learned the hard way that the most critical factor in deciding whether to accept an invitation to speak is how much I care about the attendees. If you approach an audience with that attitude, you will have an enjoyable experience, and so will the audience.

You may think it strange that I put the word "praying" in the title. I did because, for years, I was terrified to pray out loud. Today I serve on the Caring Ministry for our church. Our role is to reach out to people who are in a difficult situation, and one of the things we do is offer to pray. I've been overwhelmed to learn how much people appreciate prayer.

I was encouraged by a story told by a pastor who said he saw his little girl kneeling beside the bed saying her ABCs. When she finished, he asked her why, to which she replied: "Daddy, I didn't know what to say, but I thought God could put the letters in the right order." When I told that story to our ministry leader, she replied with this story: "Last week I was praying with someone, and I forgot their name. I was flustered, and my words felt jumbled. When I finished, the woman with whom I was praying said, 'That was the most beautiful prayer!'"

My prayer is that you will be encouraged to speak and pray whenever God gives you the opportunity!

Blessings,

Barbara

Barbara Hemphill, Founder
Productive Environment Institute
Helping Professionals Accomplish Their Work and Enjoy Their Lives!

DO YOU HAVE PURPLE POWER?

It's great to be given permission to throw this out!

Time to declutter I didn't know I had this!

From: Barbara Hemphill
Subject: Do You Have Purple Power?

If you've been around me long, you know that I love purple. When I was growing up on the farm in Nebraska, I got my own room for the first time while in high school, and I was thrilled that my mother told me I could choose what color to paint it. I chose lavender.

On the first date with my husband, Alfred, I wore a purple skirt on which he complimented me and said it was his favorite color. I have often joked that I married him because he was the first man I met who shared my love of purple. Today our house has a purple door, purple carpet, and a purple couch!

If you check out my personal website, www.BarbaraHemphill.com, you will find the theme continues in my business!

A book, written by actress Kristen Bell (*Frozen, The Good Place*), with friend and business partner Benjamin Hart, is entitled *The World Needs More Purple People*. It's a beautifully illustrated magically written book for children and adults, which outlines five steps to be a purple person:

1. Ask (really great questions)

2. Laugh (a lot)

3. Use your voice (and don't lose your voice)

4. Work hard (super-duper hard)

5. Paint yourself purple (Note: You have to read the book to find out what that means—and it will be worth your time!)

Many things about this book confirm the values, principles, and strategies Productive Environment Institute teaches. I love that it has five specific steps, just like our Productive Environment Process™:

1. State your vision.

2. Identify your obstacles.

3. Commit your resources.

4. Design and execute your plan.

5. Sustain your success.

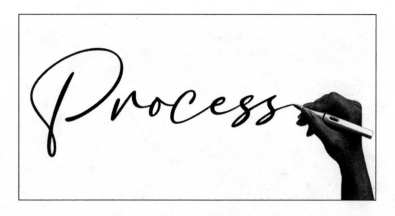

Besides, the steps to becoming a "purple person" reflect our process:

First, our coaching is about asking questions. Clients often ask us, "What should I do?" We ask, "What are you willing to do?" When a client feels stuck, one of our most frequent questions is, "What is the next action?"

Second, we love what we do. When I first started my business, I recall working with an astrophysicist. We were in the client's garage, clearing boxes of paper clutter and laughing. He stopped and said, "If anyone had ever told me I would be laughing when I cleaned out the garage, I would have told them they were crazy!"

Third, getting organized is based on creating an environment that reflects your voice. All five steps in the Productive Environment Process™ contain the word "your."

Fourth, getting organized is not easy. If it were, there wouldn't be so many millions of people watching Netflix's show "The Magic of Tidying Up," or buying (notice, I didn't say "reading") the hundreds of books on organizing! That's the bad news. The good news? Getting—and STAYING—organized will be a rewarding experience if you have a system and accountability. That's where our Certified Productive Environment Specialists™ (CPESs) come in!

Fifth—well, you have to fill out our Productive Environment Scorecard™ to find this out. www.ProductiveEnvironmentScore.com takes less than five minutes, and it might change your life forever!

Blessings,

Barbara

Barbara Hemphill, Founder
Productive Environment Institute
Helping Professionals Accomplish Their Work and Enjoy Their Lives!

WHERE ARE YOU GOING?

From: Barbara Hemphill
Subject: Where Are You Going?

When the train conductor came by, he found Albert Einstein looking in his pockets, his briefcase, and his coat for his ticket. The conductor said, "Oh, Professor Einstein. I know you, and I know you bought a ticket.

Don't worry about it." A few minutes later, when the conductor came back, Einstein was still looking. The conductor once again said, "I know you bought a ticket. Don't worry!" Einstein replied, "Oh, I know I bought a ticket. What I don't know is where I am going."

This story makes me laugh—and cry! I laugh because I often walk into a room and then stop because I don't remember why. (That's a topic for another email, I think!) I cry because there have been many times when I had no idea where I was going, and I know the Covid pandemic has caused many people in the world to have that problem. Health professionals warn that the next epidemic will be mental health issues. Suicide among teenagers alone has doubled since the beginning of Covid.

One aspect of my career that I have most enjoyed for the past 40+ years is helping people figure out where they are going. For years, I wasn't aware of the fact that was what I was doing. I thought I was helping them clear the clutter, but as the years passed, I began to see that when people were buried in physical or digital clutter, they had frequently lost their way. We always teach what we want to learn, and as I continued in my career, I realized that physical and digital clutter was a symptom of emotional clutter, which has always been a challenge for me. The crucial step in my journey was realizing that emotional clutter is a symptom of spiritual clutter.

Proverbs 29:18 (KJV) says, *"Where there is no vision, the people perish."* The Hebrew word translated "perish" or "cast off restraint" in the original means "to loosen" and thus "to expose or uncover." I find it very interesting that the act of eliminating clutter does all those things!

One reader asked me to write about "how to keep motivated when you have a lot of decluttering and organizing to do." Hundreds of people have asked that question during the years, so obviously, it's not easy. First of all, it's essential to acknowledge that organizing in and of itself has no intrinsic value! I have known people who spend much of their time organizing and reorganizing but have no tangible results, but if you know where you want to go—if you will create a vivid picture in your mind of how your organized life will be easier, more rewarding, more enjoyable, you will find the strength to keep moving forward!

Several months ago, I began the arduous process of changing my eating habits. It is, without a doubt, the most challenging change I have ever undertaken. One of my most powerful motivators is a quote from Craig Groeschel, founder of Life.Church, creator of the Bible app: *Discipline: Choosing what you want most over what you want now.* I wrote it out and posted it on the keyboard of my computer.

As a follower of Jesus, I know that where I am ultimately going is my heavenly home, but as The Lord's Prayer states, "Thy Kingdom come, Thy will be done *on earth* as it is in heaven." My passion is helping people make life *on this earth* more joyful!

If you're not sure where you are going, and you'd like to brainstorm about it, I'd be happy to offer my experience and encouragement.

You can schedule a complimentary 30-minute Discovery Session at www.ProductiveEnvironment.com

Blessings,

Barbara

Barbara Hemphill, Founder
Productive Environment Institute
Helping Professionals Accomplish Their Work and Enjoy Their Lives!

DID YOU FIND EVERYTHING?

From: Barbara Hemphill
Subject: Did You Find Everything?

When I check out at my local grocery store, the clerk asks, "Did you find everything?" Frequently, I reply (and I'm sure the clerks hears it often): "I did. More than I came for!" I have to admit that I have become a big fan of online shopping, and one of the primary reasons is that I find what I am looking for and check out. However, it's much harder to stop when I find what I'm looking for if I go into the store.

One of the principles of a "productive environment" is "You can have anything you want, but not everything." Shopping is a great example! Shopping online makes it easier to eliminate the temptation of buying more than you were shopping for—unless, of course, you get caught by the tagline, "People who bought this often buy..."

However, one of the new challenges created by online shopping is what to do with all the boxes! I keep some of them in the garage, but I often don't have the size I need when I go there to get a box. I collapse the ones I don't keep, and Alfred hauls them off to the dump along with the rest of the garbage—a task he says, "Keeps me grounded!" (The challenge of getting the product you purchased out of the packaging is a topic for another email!)

My early days as a residential organizer, the stories from colleagues in the years since, and the TV programs such as "Hoarders" reveal what I call "the evil of the big box stores." This week a friend told me about going to the home of an elderly couple who had a basement full of expired canned goods but were struggling to pay their rent.

I've always been troubled by this shopping phenomenon, but my awareness has increased in recent months. I have made friends with a family in rural India. They struggle to find even basic necessities. Because of the Covid lockdown, there is little I can do now to give them what they need.

So, here's a challenge for you to consider in the future: Before you purchase anything, ask yourself, "Is this purchase going to help me accomplish my work or enjoy my life?" If you're not sure, postpone the purchase until you are confident it will.

Blessings,

Barbara

Barbara Hemphill, Founder
Productive Environment Institute
Helping Professionals Accomplish Their Work and Enjoy Their Lives!

EMAIL 12

YOU DIDN'T MISS ANYTHING

From: Barbara Hemphill
Subject: You Didn't Miss Anything

A few readers have contacted us to say they missed my email last Sunday. I have to say I was honored to learn they noticed, but it was intentional! When I first started this project, I said I would send 30 emails in 30 days. However, last Saturday, when I was writing the email for Sunday, I suddenly realized that I didn't want to encourage reading an email on Sunday! I am an absolute believer that taking one day off from our traditional work is crucial to our well-being.

Thinking about taking Sunday off triggered me to think about the significance of vacations. According to AAA, thirty-three percent of Americans' vacation time went unused in 2020. Not only do vacations contribute to our mental health, they also can play a critical role in maintaining meaningful relationships.

One of our clients said that their family sat down in the family room and used our 5-Step Productive Environment Process™ to plan their vacation. If you don't know what that is, I invite you to do a Google search to check it out.

Several years ago, after a flood in California, the driver of my airport shuttle told me that she had just spent much of the night sandbagging her house against the deluge. And then, during the three hours it took us to get to LAX, this young woman told me an incredible story. Just two years before, she had lost everything except the clothes on her back in the earthquake. She was working alone in a trailer at a construction site. She found her way out of the door, now located above her head, by using a cigarette lighter to burn paper, so she could see to stack up furniture and climb out. She drove to her apartment to find her cousin with whom she lived, only to discover a pile of bricks. As she went around the corner, there stood her cousin, holding her dog. As they hugged, her cousin said, "I don't know how to tell you this, but you've lost everything." "No," my driver said, "I have everything I need right here!"

Her story genuinely moved me, and it reinforced my belief that one essential item on our "to do" list should be spending time with the people we love. How easy it is to think, "Oh, it's OK if I work this weekend. I'll take some time off later." The weeks and months pass, and before you know it, it may be too late.

Happy Sunday!

Blessings,

Barbara

Barbara Hemphill, Founder
Productive Environment Institute
Helping Professionals Accomplish Their Work and Enjoy Their Lives!

THE HAT: MY "LETTING GO" JOURNEY

From: Barbara Hemphill
Subject: The Hat: My "Letting Go" Journey

If you have ever been to my home, you have undoubtedly heard me say, "Everything in my environment has a story," and I would share some of the stories with you. Productive Environment Institute is all about encouraging individuals and businesses to have an "intentional setting where everyone can accomplish their work and enjoy their lives." If you haven't been to my home, but you've been around me for a while, you've undoubtedly heard me say, *Have nothing in your home you do not know to be useful, think to be beautiful—or love.* (I added the words "or love" to a quote I read from Henry Morris when I first started my organizing business.)

When Alfred and I were first married, almost 35 years ago, I quickly discovered living that philosophy in the same house would be quite a challenge! First, his tastes and "organizing style" (I use that term very loosely!) are very different from mine. At first (but not for long) I tried to keep the house "organized" to my liking, fearful that if I didn't, my business would suffer if I couldn't implement my principles in my own home. Then I realized he wasn't my client. So, we compromised. Certain parts of our house are his to do with as he will, and if you visit, it won't be difficult to see where those are, although I have to admit, through the years, his style has moved more toward mine, and mine toward his.

My home and home office have looked virtually the same for over 25 years. You'll find purple everywhere—from the front door through the piano room, the family room, and even the kitchen chairs! Tiger paraphernalia from my "paper tiger lady" days is scattered throughout (though not nearly as much as there used to be).

Throughout my life, I have spent thousands of hours and dollars on personal growth. Just after we moved into our home, I invited a Feng Shui professional to offer suggestions (regretfully, I didn't know about that before we built the house!). I loved what I learned and continue to incorporate the principles into my work to some extent. About a year ago, I enrolled in a year-long program with Dorena Kohrs (www.SpaceDoula.com), which has brought my "intentional setting journey" to a whole new level.

Raised in a very conservative Christian home, I grew up highly skeptical of practices I didn't understand. I still struggle with the fear of doing things that contradict Biblical teaching, but I have a strong belief that every culture and every discipline has something to offer. My job is to be discerning and trust what God wants for me.

Since Dorena came to my home, my journey has taken me on a whole new level of "intentional." When she asked the question, " What would you like to have?" I didn't know. I realized that I did think everything in my zone of the house "was useful, beautiful, or loved," but what I also learned was that very few items were things I had selected. Instead, they were things I had accepted.

The best illustration is a straw hat which belonged to my mother-in-law, whom I loved dearly! She was a brilliant, classy, giving woman. The hat hung on the wall over the dresser in the "Barbara Room," where I begin every morning. I thought it was lovely with dried flowers and a ribbon, and I loved looking at it and remembering Mama. It was certainly nothing I would have chosen, but the idea of letting it go made me very uncomfortable. It stayed there for several months, and then one day, I decided to take it down from the wall and put it in a closet. At my daughter-in-law's suggestion, who blesses me with unique decorating talents, my original intention was to hang it in a different part of the house according to the Bagua map. Instead, I just put it on a shelf where I couldn't see it unless I made an effort.

A few days ago, I was going through my house again with great intention to find items I could donate to Crossing All Borders Ministry (www.CrossingAllBordersMinistry.com) and saw "the hat." I realized it was a symbol of the organizing journey I am on now in which I am taking "intentional" to an entirely new level. I decided to donate the hat with a prayer of Thanksgiving for what it has meant to me.

There are several places in my home that are bare now. It felt scary at first, but it's beginning to feel very exciting. I wonder what will happen next!

Blessings,

Barbara

Barbara Hemphill, Founder
Productive Environment Institute
Helping Professionals Accomplish Their Work and Enjoy Their Lives!

THE OPPORTUNITY FOR PATIENCE

From: Barbara Hemphill
Subject: The Opportunity for Patience

Several years ago, I was on a flight from Dallas to Los Angeles when I sat next to an unaccompanied 6-year-old boy. The experience still makes me smile! We played games, talked about where he had been and where he was going. Periodically he would ask, "How much longer will it be?" I would look at my watch and give him an answer. After what seemed like the "umpteenth" time he asked, I replied, "We'll be landing soon. It just takes patience." He looked up at me with big brown innocent eyes and asked, "How long is patience?"

In this post-Covid environment, accomplishing even the most straightforward daily task is often overwhelming and requires extraordinary patience. Everyday we share horror stories about how difficult it is to get things done. I am trying to get the license plate for the car we just purchased—ironically because I wrecked the last one because of my lack of patience!

We need patience for these daily tasks, but an even more significant challenge is the challenge required to reach our dreams.

These challenging circumstances mean we have what I have decided to call an "opportunity for patience." Being patient in the most frustrating of situations is an extraordinary opportunity to express one of the most precious "fruits of the spirit," as the Bible calls such attributes.

I believe that God put each of us on earth to fulfill a purpose. In one of my favorite books, *The Dream Giver*, Bruce Wilkinson writes that each of us was given a dream when we were born, but most of us have forgotten it. In the book, he tells the story of saying that to a friend while they were in a restaurant. The friend questioned the premise, so Wilkinson said, "Let's test it out." He asked the waitress who was serving them, "Have you ever had a dream?" At first, she looked puzzled and then said, "Actually, I did. I wanted to be a nurse, but I got pregnant and became a single parent."

The dream that God gave me was to help people accomplish their work and enjoy their lives. My focus has been on encouraging people to create what I call a "productive environment"—an intentional setting in which everything around you supports who you are and who you want to be. In other ways, a setting that helps you to be all that God intended you to be. In my experience, the closer my relationship to the God who created me, the easier it is to accomplish my work and enjoy my life.

At the end of the meal at the restaurant, the waitress came back and told Wilkinson, "You know. My mother just retired, and she would be glad to take care of my daughter while I go back to school at night."

Are you living your dream? If not, what can you do to move in that direction? It will take patience, but asking the question, "What is the next action I can take?" will move you in the right direction!

Blessings,

Barbara

Barbara Hemphill, Founder
Productive Environment Institute
Helping Professionals Accomplish Their Work and Enjoy Their Lives!

THE BEGINNING OF CLUTTER

Image by Louise Wannier

From: Barbara Hemphill
Subject: The Beginning of Clutter

In my book *Less Clutter More Life* (lesscluttermorelife.com), there is an intriguing photograph of a puzzle by Louise Wannier, who did all the beautiful photographs in the book. The words with the picture say: *"Life is a puzzle. We may not know or understand how it all fits together. We may sometimes be fearful and uncertain. Unlike a physical puzzle, where we can assemble the corners and put the border pieces together first, our life puzzle is ever expanding. Anything is possible, and everything that happens is a piece in the puzzle."*

I am experiencing my life puzzle in ways that create emotions of excitement, overwhelm, and fear. I think Perry Marshall's challenge to write an email a day for 30 days was God's challenge to me to address those emotions. As a follower of Jesus, one of my biggest fears in life is offending someone. Today I am writing about what the Bible said to me, and to some readers, it may be unbelievable or even offensive, but I feel it is so profound, I must share what I heard.

As you know, eliminating clutter is the purpose and passion of my life. I started over 40 years ago helping clients eliminate physical clutter, moved on to digital clutter, and then to emotional clutter. Now I know that the foundational clutter, which creates and allows all other clutter, is spiritual.

For years, I have shared my experience that when clients are unwilling to let go of something, I will inevitably discover a hole in their heart. They are trying to fill that hole with something physical when the issue is an emotional one. Today, I am taking that premise a step further.

I have been meeting by telephone for more than three years with two dear long-time colleagues to study and discuss the Bible. This morning, we talked (as we frequently do!) about how to help a neighbor whose life is one big struggle. She spends endless hours clipping coupons from the "big box" stores and ends up buying things she doesn't need—or even use. That led to the discussion that we always try to fix our problems and our pain by adding more.

I just finished reading (and will read many more times, I'm sure) a new book by Leidy Klotz titled Subtract: The Untapped Science of Less. Dr. Klotz is a professor at the University of Virginia, with appointments in engineering, architecture, and business. Based on significant scientific studies, the book's premise is that the natural inclination of human nature is to solve problems by adding rather than subtracting.

As we were talking, God revealed to me that clutter began in the Garden of Eden. The Bible tells the story that God put Adam and Eve in the garden with everything they could need. They could have anything in it they wanted—"...BUT of the tree of the knowledge of good and evil you shall not eat, for on the day that you eat of it you shall surely die." And then came the serpent. Suddenly, Eve saw an opportunity for more, like we do. Suddenly, she was afraid that she was missing out on something, just like we are. And clutter began...

Blessings,

Barbara

Barbara Hemphill, Founder
Productive Environment Institute
Helping Professionals Accomplish Their Work and Enjoy Their Lives!

HOW DOES YOUR CLOSET LOOK?

From: Barbara Hemphill
Subject: How Does Your Closet Look?

When I started this project, I invited you to suggest topics, and some of you did. (One reader asked me to write about electric cars, but I didn't anticipate that happening!) However, two people asked about "organizing my closet." When I was thinking of a title, I thought of the children's rhyme, "Mistress Mary, quite contrary, how does your garden grow?" Hence, my title, "How Does Your Closet Look?" More importantly, is your closet a "productive environment"—an intentional setting that helps you accomplish your work and enjoy your life?

For reasons only God knows, during my quiet time today, I had the fleeting thought that there is perhaps a correlation between getting dressed for life and "putting on the whole armor of God" that we read about in Ephesians 6. I know for sure that how I dress impacts my confidence. (When I look around at what people wear these days, I realize that may mean I'm old!)

As you probably know by now, I built my business on four words: Clutter is postponed decisions.® I learned that from clothes closets. Closets are full because you have not decided to lose the ten pounds you need to lose to get in that size smaller pants you love, or what to do about the exercise equipment that looked great on Home Shopping Network, but you haven't used in years. And then there are the candlesticks from Aunt Sally. They are not your style, but Aunt Sally would be so thrilled to see them on the table when she comes for Thanksgiving—if you can find them.

Here are seven stumbling blocks that prevent people from making their clothes closet a place they love:

1. I don't know where to begin.

2. I don't have time to deal with it.

3. I don't have enough space.

4. I can't wear some of the clothes now, but I'm planning to lose weight.

5. I feel guilty because I haven't even worn some of the clothes.

6. I know I could give them away, but I want them to be appreciated.

7. I'm not sure how to do it.

I don't know where to begin.

As it says in Proverbs, "Without a vision, the people perish." If your closet were a place that you enjoyed using, how would it look? "I could bring my girlfriend in to show her my new shoes with no apologies!" What would you be able to do that you can't do now? "I could find what I wanted to wear in a few minutes." What wouldn't happen that happens now? "I wouldn't have to iron so often because of unnecessary wrinkles."

So, here's one idea: Put an easily accessible clipboard or notebook with a pen in your closet. Every time you see or experience something you don't like in your closet, jot it down. (You don't need the solution here— just the problem.) When you think of something you would like, jot that down too!

I don't have time to deal with it.

As the old saying goes, "Pay me now or pay me later." Based on my experience, you can organize the average closet in four hours. How long does it take you to find the clothes you want to wear each morning or to iron the skirt that you wouldn't have had to iron if you had hung it up when you took it out of the dryer?

There are two ways you can approach organizing your closet:

1.   Block out a Saturday morning and "just do it"!

2. Work on it 15 minutes at a time until you get it done (it will take longer than four hours if you do it in increments). Design a specific plan for what you will do in those 15-minute increments.

I don't have enough space.

If your closet is disorganized, you can't tell if you have enough space. Consider what I call The Cost Factor™: "You can keep everything you want if you're willing to pay the price: time, space, energy, and money." Research shows that 80% of what we keep we never use. If it turns out you don't have enough space, there are solutions for that too, but don't use lack of space as an excuse until you know the facts.

I can't wear some of these clothes now, but I'm planning on losing weight.

Really? How long has that been going on? And, if you did, are you sure you'd want to wear those clothes? But let's go back to The Cost Factor™. If you have plenty of space, there's not a problem, but if you can't hang up today's dry cleaning because of something you haven't worn for five years...well, you get the point!

I haven't even worn some of these clothes.

I'll never forget the day I was helping a woman clean out her closet, and I asked her, "How does this dress make you feel?" She looked at me, and her face dropped down as she replied, "Guilty." My response: "If anything in your closet creates a negative emotion—e.g., sad, guilty, fat—you can't afford it!"

I know I could give them away, but I want someone to handle them responsibly.

Keeping items for "someday" when there are undoubtedly people 30 minutes from your house that need it today is not good stewardship. Volunteer or take a tour to find a donor organization you want to support.

I'm not sure how to do it.

To start with, you don't have to do it alone. You likely have a friend for whom organizing closets is fun, and if you're willing to get over your embarrassment, she would love to help you. If you're not comfortable doing that, invest in yourself, hire someone who can help, and more importantly, teach you the skill so you can do it yourself the next time.

Walking into an intentional environment in your closet will positively impact your day every day!

Blessings,

Barbara

Barbara Hemphill, Founder
Productive Environment Institute
Helping Professionals Accomplish Their Work and Enjoy Their Lives!

ANOTHER CLOSET LESSON: THE NEED FOR MARGIN

From: Barbara Hemphill
Subject: Another Closet Lesson: The Need for Margin

Yesterday I wrote about organizing your closet. This morning, I realized that I forgot one critical rule if you are organizing that closet (or any area of your home or office, for that matter) in short segments: For every hour of organizing, allow ten minutes for "clean up."

Do you recognize this scenario? You start organizing the closet and find something that belongs in the laundry room. You notice several things there that shouldn't be, and before you realize it, you've spent 15 minutes in the laundry room, with no progress in the closet where you started, and it's time to leave for soccer practice!

Next time, focus on the closet. (You would be well-served to bring a trash bag and a box for donations.) Set your alarm to remind you to allow ten minutes for each hour of organizing. If you find something that belongs somewhere else, start a pile for each location. When the alarm rings, take the piles to their appropriate place. (At that point, you may realize that you need to organize that area too! Take a deep breath. That project is for another day.)

One of the significant challenges of life in this century is our unwillingness to allow what author Richard A. Swenson writes about in one of my favorite books, *Margin: Restoring Emotional, Physical, Financial, and Time Reserves to Overloaded Lives.* We need margin! This malady shows up in our closet organizing project in two ways. We don't allow physical margin in the closet, nor do we allow time margin to manage what we keep.

Swenson writes: "*We have more 'things per person' than any other nation in history. Closets are full, storage space is used up, and cars can't fit into garages.*" He goes on to say, "*Our love affair with plastic is one of the main reasons we have 'no room to wiggle,' that is, no margin.*" When you read the word "plastic," you may immediately think of storage containers in your kitchen or the recycle bin, but what about all the plastic in your closet? Indeed, solving this universal problem is going to require creativity and innovation.

Last week I learned about Tom Cridland, who has just launched the world's first-ever collection of sustainable clothing backed by a 30-year guarantee! His goal is to help lead the fashion industry trend toward protecting our natural resources. That's certainly a step in the right direction, and I ordered a shirt with a tiger on it. This "Paper Tiger Lady" couldn't resist! That brings up the next step: changing our buying habits.

Perhaps that's a topic for another day! In the meantime, give some thought to this question: Where do you need margin?

As we approach another weekend, consider additional observation from Swenson: "*We do not rest because our work is done; we rest because God commanded it and created us to have a need for it.*"

Blessings,

Barbara

Barbara Hemphill, Founder
Productive Environment Institute
Helping Professionals Accomplish Their Work and Enjoy Their Lives!

EMAIL 18

PESTS AND GRATITUDE

From: Barbara Hemphill
Subject: Pests and Gratitude

I never thought I would use the words "gratitude" and "pests" in the same sentence, but my recent experience with a local pest control company has made it possible.

Today when I came home from a meeting, I found a "Sorry we missed you!" door hanger from Sustainable Pest Systems. A few years ago, I met Peter Rubino, a sales rep for Sustainable Pest Systems (SPS), at a networking meeting. At the time, we had a contract with a company we had used for over two decades, but I put Peter's name in my database.

Last year, the company we used was bought out by another company, and as is often the case in mergers and acquisitions, the result was not good news for the customer. I recalled my conversation with Peter and gave him a call. He referred me to the office, and we signed a contract. It has been a most rewarding relationship—not only because we don't have any "pests," but because every interaction with the company has been professional and enjoyable.

Here are four reasons doing business with SPS is such a great experience:

1.   The contract is easy-to-understand and reasonably priced.

2.   They deliver the services for which we paid, on time and without prompting.

3.   The office staff answers my questions with kindness and facts.

4.   The technicians communicate politely and clearly when they are coming.

In one of his coaching classes, Dan Sullivan, founder of The Strategic Coach®, shared what he called "The Four Referability Habits." He said that if an entrepreneur did these four things, they would be ahead of 80% of the rest of the businesses:

1.   Show up on time.

2.   Do what you say you will do.

3.   Finish what you start.

4.   Say "please" and "thank you."

SPS does those four things and more, and for that reason, I can comfortably put "pest" and "gratitude" together!

Blessings,

Barbara

Barbara Hemphill, Founder
Productive Environment Institute
Helping Professionals Accomplish Their Work and Enjoy Their Lives!

WE'RE ALL DYING, BUT ARE WE LIVING?

From: Barbara Hemphill
Subject: We're All Dying, But Are We Living?

My husband's Uncle Herbert died during a speech he was giving at his Rotary Club. I hope I am that blessed! Like Uncle Herbert, I want to die living rather than live dying!

That brings up the big question: What is "living" to you? Ikigai (pronounced *ee-key-guy*) is a beautiful Japanese concept that essentially means "a reason for being." Combine two Japanese words: *iki*, meaning "life," and *kai*, meaning "effect, result, worth, or benefit," and you get: "a reason for living."

There are a few people in the world, far too few, in my experience, who live life in such a way that you love being around them—hoping that perhaps some of their joy will rub off on you!

Joy has not come easy for me. As I have shared in previous writing, depression has haunted my life. I prayed for peace from that depression for years, and I'm happy to report, I found it—at least most of the time! Finding joy is more challenging. Notice I said "is" because it's not yet my constant state of mind. But as my first mother-in-law, an amazing woman who was a polio survivor, a mother of seven, and a teacher of children with special needs, regularly said: *"Every day in every way I'm getting better and better!"*

A few weeks ago, I felt particularly sorrowful about the state of the world, our country, and many people I know worldwide who are suffering in various ways. When I shared my feelings with Judy Greenman, founder of Body Brain Freedom (bbfree.com) who is one of the most joyous people I know, she asked a question: *"When you feel sad, what is your focus?"* I paused and then had to admit (sheepishly) that the answer was "Me."

She then followed up with another question, "How does your feeling sad make anything better?" Some exploration revealed that my sadness was a result of guilt for all the blessings I have. Again she asked a poignant question: "How does your feeling guilty help anyone else?" I suddenly realized that not only did my guilt not help them, but it also added a layer of unnecessary responsibility to their challenges because they couldn't help me. That realization drives me with a deep desire to live joyfully!

There's an old gospel song that puts it well:

> *The joy of the Lord is my strength*
> *The joy of the Lord is my strength*
> *In the darkness I'll dance*
> *In the shadows I'll sing*
> *The joy of the Lord is my strength*

We are all looking for meaning and purpose in life. We are searching for a reason to live. If you're not sure, start by paying attention to what brings you joy—and be intentional about figuring out how to do more of it. Not only will you feel more joyful, so will the people around you. As Abraham Lincoln put it so well, *"And in the end, it's not the years in your life that count. It's the life in your years."*

Blessings,

Barbara

Barbara Hemphill, Founder
Productive Environment Institute
Helping Professionals Accomplish Their Work and Enjoy Their Lives!

WHO ARE YOU?

From: Barbara Hemphill
Subject: Who Are You?

The CSI theme song "Who Are You?" is a highly challenging question in this season of Covid. In an episode of the TV show "The Good Doctor," Dr. Murphy, played by Freddie Highmore, told his friend, "We are the decisions we make, and you let other people make them for you, so you're not being anyone." I rarely make notes from TV shows, but that statement struck me as *truth!*

"Clutter is postponed decisions®" is the founding principle of Productive Environment Institute (PEI). The premise of my book *Less Clutter More Life* (lesscl48uttermorelife.com) is that physical and digital clutter is a symptom of emotional and spiritual clutter. Living our lives based on other people's needs results in emotional clutter and creates "spiritual clutter"—not being what God created us to be.

In our Covid-19 world, there are many times when it is appropriate and loving to put other people's needs before ourselves, but too often, we do it when it is unnecessary—or even unhelpful in the long run. I know that scenario well because I've lived much of my life afraid of other people's anger or even displeasure. It's taken years of therapy, counseling, Bible study, and prayer to gain the emotional strength to ask myself, "Who am I?" and try to live out the answer.

Now, because of Covid-19, many people have more decisions to make about who they are and what they should be doing than ever before, so I'd like to make two suggestions:

1. **Ask yourself, "Who am I?"**

    To put it another way, "Who did God create me to be?" It's not a simple question, and if you're like me, it may take years to answer, and it undoubtedly will change as your circumstances change, but it's not a question to ignore. As you get clear about who you are, it's easier to decide what you should do.

You may have heard me say that I would like on my tombstone (which will only have the ashes left from the donation of my body to research), "She gave others hope." I want everything I do to bring hope to others, which can come in many forms. My business partner Andrea Anderson came up with the acronym HOPE: Help Others Pursue Entrepreneurship, which is the purpose of our Certified Productive Environment Specialist™ (CPES™) program. First, they become entrepreneurs, and then they enable others to do the same. I want every conversation to offer hope, and I love to share my ultimate hope in Jesus Christ.

2. **Create structure and accountability in your life.**

    In the absence of structure and accountability, I will fritter away the gift of time. Research shows I am 64% more likely to accomplish a goal if I have an accountability partner. Here's the irony: asking for help means admitting my weakness, but when I take that risk, I encourage others to do the same. God designed us to live life together so everyone can accomplish their work and enjoy their lives. Together we are better!

Blessings,

Barbara

Barbara Hemphill, Founder
Productive Environment Institute
Helping Professionals Accomplish Their Work and Enjoy Their Lives!

WHAT IS "ORGANIZED"?

From: Barbara Hemphill
Subject: What is "Organized"?

Many people assume that since I have been a professional productivity and organizing consultant for over forty years, I am "naturally organized." The people who live and work with me would confirm that is not true! That's why I'm good at what I do—I don't have any difficulty understanding why people need organizing services. I consistently get experience tackling new challenges in my own life and those of my clients.

So you may wonder, "How did you end up in the organizing profession?" I had the incredible advantage of growing up on a Nebraska farm where my family was "organization in action." Although the house certainly wasn't always tidy, we could accomplish our work because my parents role-modeled organization. I can still hear my mother saying, "If you're going upstairs, take something with you." She always set the clock in our kitchen five minutes fast. I never understood why that worked, but it certainly impressed upon me the value of being on time. I can still see my father quickly washing the car on Sunday morning before driving to church! Getting organized enables you to accomplish what you value.

Many people assume that I am a "neat freak"—or that I live by the principle of "Handle a piece of paper only once!" If that were necessary, I would be in serious trouble. Often people see me and say, "I could never be like you," and dismiss the possibility that there are other ways to get organized. God created each of us with a unique DNA, and it is my experience that we each organize differently. Organizing is an art. There is no "right" or "wrong" way.

To determine whether something in my life is organized, I continually ask four simple questions:

1. **Does it work?**

    To put it simply, "Am I able to do what I want to do?"

2. **Do I like it?**

   That question always reminds me of a CFO for a movie production company who said, "I'd like to have a clean desk, but every time I do, I can't find anything!" After experiencing our "Total Office Transformation," he liked the way his desk looked—AND he could find what he wanted.

3. **Does it work for the people it impacts?**

   That is undoubtedly the most significant challenge—at home and work. My marriage is more important to me than a clutter-free home. Compromise is essential, but I've learned that when I'm feeling frustrated by my husband's clutter, it helps to clean up my own! I often remind employees that the information they manage belongs to the organization. It is their responsibility to organize it so that others can find it when necessary.

4. **How quickly can you recover?**

   Let's face it. Life is messy. Despite your best plans, disorganization happens. People get sick. Airline flights are canceled. Projects fail. People don't do what they said they would. But recovering is significantly more manageable when I am organized!

Two questions we encourage clients to answer:

1. How much clutter are you willing to tolerate?

2. How much time are you willing to devote to cleaning it up? During the middle of the week, you will probably find my home or office in a disorganized state, but I clean it up once a week. If it takes longer than 30 minutes, I know it's time for some reorganization!

There are always areas of life I want to organize more effectively, but using these questions keeps helping me improve.

Blessings,

Barbara

Barbara Hemphill, Founder
Productive Environment Institute
Helping Professionals Accomplish Their Work and Enjoy Their Lives!

EMAIL 22

WHAT DISTRACTS YOU?

From: Barbara Hemphill
Subject: What Distracts You?

A 2021 study revealed that the average person checks their cell phone 58 times a day. Talk about a distraction! Many clients have been diagnosed with ADHD (as have I), but regardless, we live in an ADHD world. Distractions are everywhere! Isn't it interesting that virtually all media has built-in distractions? (Perhaps it began when television introduced the "crawl line" at the bottom of the screen.)

Distractions are a form of clutter! Sometimes something we intended as a positive ends up being a distraction. For over three decades, I had a close relationship with a friend. Throughout the years, I collected evidence of that relationship which I displayed throughout my home. Last year, due to the lessons I've learned from Feng Shui, which I have talked about previously, I realized that many of those items were a distraction because I felt sad every time I looked at them since we no longer communicate.

Several of the gifts were there because of our relationship, not because they were something I would have chosen, so I donated them. One of them was a beautifully framed photo of dried flowers, which I love. It remains.

One of the fundamental principles of Productive Environment Institute is, "Often you have to give up *good* to get *best.*" *Good* is often a distraction.

In Luke, we read about Jesus visiting Mary and Martha: Mary sat at the Lord's feet and listened to his teaching. But Martha was distracted with much serving. And she went up to him and said, *"Lord, do you not care that my sister has left me to serve alone? Tell her to help me."* But the Lord answered her, *"Martha, Martha, you are anxious and troubled about many things, but one thing is necessary. Mary has chosen the good portion, which will not be taken from her."* How I struggle with that admonition!

I read a story of Martin Luther, who said, *"I have so much to do today that I'm going to need to spend three hours in prayer to be able to get it all done."* That may sound ludicrous, but it took me decades to realize that the more time I spend in prayer, the more peace I feel and the more I accomplish. The only explanation? Isaiah 55:6 (NIV) has this answer: *"For my thoughts are not your thoughts, neither are your ways my ways, declares the Lord."*

What distracts you? Here's a challenge to consider: Identify one "good" distraction and put a plan in place to replace it with "best!"

Blessings,

Barbara

Barbara Hemphill, Founder
Productive Environment Institute
Helping Professionals Accomplish Their Work and Enjoy Their Lives!

WHAT ABOUT ALL MY "STUFF"?

From: Barbara Hemphill
Subject: What About All My "Stuff"?

I have previously written about my mother-in-law, a polio survivor, mother of seven children, and teacher of children with special needs. One of her many memorable phrases was: "Finish in style." I don't recall what situation initially prompted that statement, but I think it's wise advice for those of us who have accumulated a lifetime of "stuff."

It happened twice recently. The first time, I was shopping with a friend who mentioned to the clerk, "Barbara helps people eliminate clutter." Without a moment's hesitation, the clerk began a 30-minute diatribe about her struggle with all the "stuff" she inherited from her mother. Two days later, I was speaking at a Rotary Club on the topic of "The Cultural Impact of Clutter in Our Post-Covid World." (That was before we understood the impact of the new Covid strain!) I spent most of my time talking about the clutter in business, but when it came time for Q&A, most of the questions were about "inherited clutter."

The situation is a very emotional one.

Research shows, and I've repeatedly confirmed in my life and the lives of my clients in the past 40+ years, that 80% of what we keep we never use. Furthermore, the more we have, the less we use—either because we don't remember we have it, we can't find it, or it's too difficult to access, but we save it.

The situation is further complicated in today's world as we learn that our children and grandchildren have little or no interest in all the "stuff" we've accumulated during our lifetime. This lack of interest in what we did with our lives prompts the emotional question, "Did my life matter?" At a seminar I presented on downsizing in a retirement community, I suggested that people ask their children what specific items they would like to have. One gentleman replied, "The only thing my son wants is my wallet!" There were many knowing laughs.

While you may think this is a new problem, I discovered in my research for my latest book, *Less Clutter More Life* (lessclruttermorelife.com), that it's been around a long time. In the King James Version of the Bible, in 1 Samuel 10:22, Samuel is looking for Saul to appoint him king, but can't find him. When he asks the Lord about it, we see this reply: "And the Lord answered, behold he hath hid himself among the stuff."

So what DO you do with all that "stuff" that has accumulated? Here are three ways you can get started:

1. Begin creating and maintaining a list of agencies, organizations, and even businesses that will take what you don't need and recycle or repurpose. For example, those towels that have been around forever would be welcome at an animal shelter. Check your pantry shelves periodically for canned goods you don't use and donate them to a food pantry before the expiration date.

2. Identify a permanent location or container—clearly labeled—in your home where you can quickly put things you don't need or want anymore. If you have more than one floor, have a location or container on each floor. Create a reminder to deliver donations regularly.

3. Begin looking at your belongings to determine whether they really will help you "finish in style" by asking the question: "Does this help me accomplish my work or enjoy my life?" If the answer is, "Not really," it's clutter. Make it someone else's blessing—and live happily ever after!

I can't count the hours I have spent with clients struggling with deep emotion, grieving over losing someone they love, and feeling disrespectful because they are getting rid of their stuff. So my most important advice: If you cannot or do not want to get rid of the things you have collected in your lifetime, tell your children that whatever they do with your belongings when you are gone is fine. That, dear reader, is a way to "Finish in style!"

Blessings,

Barbara

Barbara Hemphill, Founder
Productive Environment Institute
Helping Professionals Accomplish Their Work and Enjoy Their Lives!

EMAIL 24

I'M NOT QUITTING!

From: Barbara Hemphill
Subject: I'm Not Quitting!

It's "Day 24" of my 30-day email series! I so enjoyed writing the first 22, but the last few have been a different story. Whenever I have an idea for a new email or blog, I start writing on the Grammarly platform. I have many "starts," but getting to "finished" has been a significant challenge for the past few days.

My intention in these 30 emails is to encourage my readers, but today is one of those days when I need encouragement. I shared that with my business coach today, and she said many of her colleagues and clients are feeling discouraged these days and suggested that I write about it, so here goes!

I could cite many reasons for my feelings, but I'm confident that a significant contributor is the resurgence of Covid and the uncertain future we face. While the truth is "Clutter is postponed decisions®," Covid gives me a reason, and in some cases, an excuse, for not deciding about anything!

Throughout this series, I have shared the principles of Productive Environment Institute, which I am confident that I have learned to teach others. One of those we call "The Next Action Factor™." I often get "stuck" and am tempted to quit, but when that happens, I try to identify one thing I want to accomplish and ask the critical question, "What is the *next* action I need to take to accomplish this goal?"

Often the answer to that question involves an *ask*. Asking is never easy for me (and I know from experience with clients that I am not alone!), and when I am feeling discouraged, it's overwhelming. My husband taught me an exercise to do with audiences that illustrates how ridiculous that is! I invite everyone in the audience to find a partner. One person is "A," and the other is "B." The exercise is for "A" to make a fist and for "B" to try to get it open. (Of course, I state all kinds of warnings such as "Don't participate if you have a bad shoulder," and "You have to promise to stop when I say 'Stop!'") It's humorous to watch the antics teams perform to get results, but it only takes a few seconds to see some are successful, so we stop. I then ask the team with an open fist, "How did you do it?" The answer is simple: "I asked my partner, 'Will you please open your fist?'"

Finally, one strategy that I can always count on to help move me forward is music! So before I started this email, I put on music (instrumental only for me, please). So, my task is complete.

Thank you for listening to my *rant*! As a "philosopher" Vince Lombardi put it so succinctly, "*Winners never quit, and quitters never win.*" I don't know what you're trying to accomplish that feels overwhelming, but I'm *not quitting*, and I hope you won't either!

Blessings,

Barbara

Barbara Hemphill, Founder
Productive Environment Institute
Helping Professionals Accomplish Their Work and Enjoy Their Lives!

EMAIL 25

ANGER

From: Barbara Hemphill
Subject: Anger

One of my greatest treasures is the Global Impact Bible given to me in 2018 when I attended a conference at the Museum of the Bible in Washington, D.C. It contains beautifully illustrated stories that tell how Biblical principles have impacted world culture throughout history. I use it most mornings during my quiet time, and often those stories point to lessons I feel God is teaching me. This morning was one of those!

I grew up in a family that admired President Eisenhower. Many years ago, I traveled to Pennsylvania to help a family member decide how to handle the family's belongings after the death of Mamie Eisenhower. I had a wonderful time, and the extraordinary experience strengthened my admiration for him and his family.

I'm always amazed at how what I read in my morning quiet time seems poignantly applicable to American life. Today in the Global Impact Bible, there was a story about President Eisenhower based on Proverbs 16:32 (NIV), which reads "*Whoever is slow to anger is better than the mighty; and he who rules his (own) spirit than he who takes a city.*"

Here is an excerpt from that story:

> As a child, Eisenhower wanted to join his two older brothers for trick-or-treating at Halloween. His parents told him he was too young to go. The young Eisenhower had a temper tantrum and was sent to his room. Eisenhower describes the story: "Perhaps an hour later, my mother came into the room. I was still sobbing into the pillow...She began to talk about temper and controlling it. Eventually, as she often did, she drew on the Bible...'Hatred was a futile sort of thing,' she said, 'because hating anyone or anything means that there was little to be gained. The person who had incurred the displeasure probably didn't care, possibly didn't even know, and the only person injured was myself.' I have always looked back on that conversation as one of the most valuable moments of my life."

Of course, as I contemplated what I read, I thought of America. Indeed, America is full of anger today, and we can see the results everywhere, but what struck me this morning was more personal.

In my last email about my recent struggle in writing these emails, I didn't share the reason. I'm not sure I was even aware of the cause at that point, but it is evident to me after reading the Eisenhower story.

I have a plaque hanging in my kitchen that reads, *"Marriages are not made in heaven. They come in kits and you have to put them together."*

If I had been creating that plaque, I would have added, *"over and over again."* The past few days have been one of those times.

Ephesians 4:26 (KJV) says, *"Be angry and sin not!"* My challenge, and I believe the challenge in our country, is figuring out when anger is appropriate because the truth is being ignored but sharing that truth in a Godly manner.

One of my "go-to" verses in the Bible is Lamentations 3:22-23 (NIV), which reads, *"Because of the Lord's great love we are not consumed, for his compassions never fail. They are new every morning; great is your faithfulness."* I am thankful that this morning, a Monday morning at that, is here, and I will try again to see Alfred's point of view—and God's!

Blessings,

Barbara

Barbara Hemphill, Founder
Productive Environment Institute
Helping Professionals Accomplish Their Work and Enjoy Their Lives!

TAMING THE (YOUR)
EMAIL TIGER

From: Barbara Hemphill
Subject: Taming the (Your) Email Tiger

With only five days remaining in my 30-day Email Project, I have been deeply considering what topics I want to be sure to include. As I pondered what questions people most often ask me, I concluded there were two:

1. What do I do about all the "stuff" in my house that came from other people? (I will address that topic tomorrow!)

2. How do you handle all your email? As you can see, that's my topic for today.

Notice in the title of this email, I very intentionally included the words "the" and "your." My reason for this choice is that email is a very serious problem on two levels: individual and organizational.

The foundational principle of Productive Environment Institute (PEI), **Clutter is postponed decisions®,** certainly applies to email. It's so easy to start my day with a glance at email on my phone or my Mac, followed by "open," "close," "open," "close," and before I know it, 40 minutes have gone by, and nothing has changed—except my mood when I realize how much I have to do!

Many other principles of PEI apply to this topic:

- **"Control what you can, so you can cope with what you can't."**

  That admonition certainly applies to the email you receive.

- **Today's mail is tomorrow's pile™.**

  If you have learned what we teach about paper—that is, ignore the old piles and stop the problem—it applies to email as well.

- **The Cost Factor™**

  You can keep everything you want if you are willing to pay the price in time, space, money, and energy.

- **Half of any job is using the right tool**

Few email users utilize all the built-in tools of their email provider.

- **Continually apply the Art of Wastebasketry® question**

  What's the worst thing that would happen if I deleted/unsubscribed from this email? If you can live with your answer, do it!

A March 2021 survey of 1,000 office professionals currently working from home found:

- Eighty-six percent said that sorting through their inbox is one of the most unpleasant parts of work.

- Thirty-eight percent said that "email fatigue" is likely to push them to quit their jobs. (Among workers 40 and under the percentage was 51%)

- Fifty percent spent their own money on tools to help manage their productivity.

The solution to this problem lies with management. Happily, based on my experience with clients, leaders can address the email problem quickly with a small financial investment compared to the cost of the problem with two initiatives:

1. An Email Protocol Program
2. Training

If you are a Gmail user, I highly recommend you invest in the publication published early this year by Certified Productive Environment Specialist™ (CPES™) Judith Guertin, in collaboration with Yours Truly, called *Taming the Digital Tiger: Gmail Edition.* It's available on Amazon in paper format (beautifully formatted and easy to read) and in digital format. Designed as a reference book, keep it readily available to get quick answers!

Our friend Prasanth Nair, founder of Double Gemini, created "The Stack Method™" for taking control of your email. His philosophies are in line with the teachings of Productive Environment Institute, and we're grateful that he has permitted us to share his high-quality masterclass with our community. Here is the link: bit.ly/thestackmethod

Happy email taming!

Blessings,

Barbara

Barbara Hemphill, Founder
Productive Environment Institute
Helping Professionals Accomplish Their Work and Enjoy Their Lives!

OTHER PEOPLE'S CLUTTER

From: Barbara Hemphill
Subject: Other People's Clutter

My passion is living an intentional life—and encouraging others to do the same! My company, Productive Environment Institute, defines "productive environment" as "an intentional setting in which everyone can accomplish their work and enjoy their lives."

In my 40+ year journey in the organizing and productivity industry, I have observed that one of the biggest obstacles to "intentional" is clutter. I first saw it in clothes closets, which led to the foundational principle "Clutter is Postponed Decisions®." Stuffed closets existed because clients hadn't decided whether they were serious about losing 20 pounds so they could wear that favorite pair of pants. Soon, I realized that the biggest clutter challenge was (and in many instances, still is!) paper. The result of that "aha" was my first book *Taming the Paper Tiger* (now called *Organizing Paper @ Home: What to Keep and How to Find the Rest!*, written in collaboration with Jennifer Wig Suarez). Then came digital clutter—especially email (which I wrote about yesterday).

As I worked with clients to eliminate physical and digital clutter, I realized that the cause was much more profound: emotional clutter. Whenever I had a client who struggled to decide whether to keep something, I would ask questions. Inevitably, the struggle related to the emotional issues I wrote about in *Less Clutter More Life: A Life's Teaching* (lessclluttermorelife.com), beautifully illustrated by Louise Wannier.

I shared in a previous email some suggestions for how to handle your clutter, but a big clutter issue that plagues American society today is "Other People's Clutter." (I'm not an expert about the problem in other cultures, but I have heard stories from colleagues that we are not alone in the challenge.)

Perhaps the problem began during The Great Depression. I read a story about Eleanor Roosevelt. When she died, they found a piece of cardboard wrapped in string with a note attached: "Bits of string too small to be saved." Today, I hear story after story from people whose relatives lived in that era and died, leaving houses full of worthless items mingled with potentially valuable items.

At an event where I spoke, a gentleman sadly shared a story of boxes of inherited items they had moved from one house to another that his wife had never opened.

Today, friends, colleagues, and clients share the sadness that the beautiful, meaningful items we collected during our lifetime to give to our children and grandchildren are of no interest. We then face the emotional question: "Did my life matter to anyone else?"

If you have inherited someone else's clutter, here are four steps one of my clients wisely took with her mother's house:

1. Since her siblings wanted nothing to do with her mom's belongings, she identified what items she wanted that would help her "accomplish her work or enjoy her life."

2. She created an event and invited her mother's friends to come to the house and choose one item they would like as a remembrance. It was a lovely evening of remembrance.

3. She invited an expert to come to the house to identify items of financial value.

4. She invited charities to come and take what they could use, including one that would take anything that remained.

Other people's clutter is often an issue at work, as well. One client complained, *"At work, people give me stuff I have to keep; I don't have a choice. And at home, other people's stuff drives me crazy."* I challenged my client on "I have to keep." After some research about records retention in her industry, we were able to get rid of her clutter and inspire her colleagues to do the same!

The shortest path to frustration and failure is trying to change other people. Tell yourself a new story about the extraordinary level of power and control you have over one person in the universe—you. Say to yourself, "I won't allow anything to rob me of my freedom to create the results I want in my life." In other words, change what you can (*you*), accept what you cannot change (*everyone else*), and waste no energy fighting over the difference. (I've never forgotten a story I read about a prisoner of war who was assigned to work knee-deep in sewage. Instead of feeling sorry for himself, since he had no control over the situation, he imagined being there alone with God and sang the song, *I Come to the Garden Alone*.)

Very few people are truly impervious to their environment. Some of us pretend we are. We make promises to take care of the clutter later. In the meantime, we walk around as incomplete, diminished versions of the fully resourceful, fully generous people we could be. The world needs the best you have to give, and if you smother your best in clutter, we all lose.

Blessings,

Barbara

Barbara Hemphill, Founder
Productive Environment Institute
Helping Professionals Accomplish Their Work and Enjoy Their Lives!

DO SOMETHING!

From: Barbara Hemphill
Subject: Do Something!

I love to read, but doing so often creates a challenge for me because knowledge creates options, and options require decisions, and making a decision can create fear. So what happens? I do nothing! What happens then? Nothing!

Clients often ask us, "What should I do?" Our answer: "That's the wrong question! The important question is 'What WILL you do?'"

Thirty years ago, Stephen Covey came to North Carolina to present his newly released book *7 Habits of Highly Effective People*. The impact on my life was immeasurable.

First, he began his presentation by asking us to hold up our right hand and promise to share something we learned from his presentation within the next 48 hours. I discovered something from that experience relevant to something I am learning from this "Email a Day for 30 Days" experience. I listened differently to what Covey had to say, knowing that I would have to share it. I've discovered that my entire life is more interesting when I live it thinking about what I want to share in my next email!

Secondly, Covey challenged us to "Name one thing that would improve the quality of your life." My answer was immediate: EXERCISE. I wasn't overweight, but I was certainly out of shape, and I left that hotel ballroom determined to do something about it. My first attempt was an exercise bicycle, which turned out to be a great place to hang my dirty clothes. My second attempt was a treadmill. It turned out to be a great place to pack my suitcase! Then I met Dave Hubbard, who introduced me to a program that used equipment I could carry in my suitcase, do in my hotel room, and only required 10 minutes/day! Suddenly all my excuses were gone, and I did it for over 20 years. Since then, I've tried a variety of exercise options, but I'm always doing something!

I read a recent study about exercise which revealed that working out in the evening may be better for the body than exercising in the morning. It's easy to make excuses about why something won't work, but who would argue that exercise is vital, and the options are endless. So, if you need to exercise, the question is, "What WILL you do?"

The admonition, "Do something!" applies to anything you want to improve in your life, whether it is your health, a new job, or a relationship with someone important to you.

So here's my two-question challenge for today:

1. What is one thing that has to happen for you to be happy with your progress?

2. What is something you can do today to move in that direction? If it doesn't work, you've learned something, and you can do something else!

Blessings,

Barbara

Barbara Hemphill, Founder
Productive Environment Institute
Helping Professionals Accomplish Their Work and Enjoy Their Lives!

GOD IS AT WORK BIGTIME!

From: Barbara Hemphill
Subject: God is at Work BIGTIME!

Hello from Andrea! For Barbara's 29th email, I get to share on her behalf! When I was a child, my mom had a sign in the kitchen that read *Life is what happens to us while we are making other plans!* That is the case with Barbara today, and she has asked me to bring you up to date on her latest adventure!

While *Enjoying Her Life* on horseback yesterday, there was a mishap that landed her in the hospital with a broken clavicle. True to her nature, she makes lemonade out of lemons! Here's her message to our team:

> *"God is at work BIGTIME! I'm home from the hospital. I have a broken clavicle. One bone is stacked on the other, so it will probably require surgery, but they can't do that until the swelling goes down. I have appt with an orthopedic surgeon Nov 16. We are still going on vacation—sure will be easy to pack since I can't move my shoulder or my elbow!*
>
> *This week I have been handing out invitations to a Community Celebration our church is hosting to honor first responders, fire fighters, and EM providers. I had ONE invitation left in my car, which I put in my hand and gave to one of the EMS techs who helped me in the ambulance!"*

Only Barbara! :)

We ask that you keep Barbara in your thoughts and prayers as she is healing. She will be back stronger than ever with the final email, Day 30! I guess she thought she needed a new story to share!

Cheers,

Andrea

Andrea Anderson, CEO
Productive Environment Institute

IT ISN'T THE END YET...

From: Barbara Hemphill
Subject: It Isn't the End Yet...

I was very reticent to start this "30 Emails in 30 Days" assignment because I am famous for creating projects I don't finish! It turned out to be one of the most challenging and enjoyable projects I have undertaken. I completed Day 28, but the next day I had a horseback riding accident and broke my collarbone. My right arm was in a sling, which made it difficult to use my computer, and the pain caused my creativity to plummet, so the project came to a screeching halt.

Another of my intentions for the year was to write a book to celebrate my 75th birthday. I had many ideas, had discussed them with a publisher, and started writing, but that project also came to a halt. A few weeks before my birthday, I shared with my Productive Environment Institute team that my biggest regret for the year was that I didn't accomplish that goal.

On my birthday, the Productive Environment team planned a virtual birthday party. Andrea Anderson, CEO, said, *"Barbara, you told us you wanted to write a book for your 75th birthday, and we want to show you that you did!"* And much to my amazement, they presented a beautifully designed, 75-page book consisting of the 29 emails I had written. It is undoubtedly one of the most loving, surprising, and creative birthday gifts I have ever received.

Several of the principles that Productive Environment Institute teaches—what Laura Morgan, PEI Director of Business Development, calls " Barbara-isms"—apply to this story:

- Yesterday's mess can become tomorrow's message.

- As in music, your life is as much about the notes you leave out as the ones you put in.

- You can have anything you want, but not everything.

- Every day in every way, I'm getting better and better. (Learned that from my mother in-law, a polio survivor.)

- Expect the best, take what comes with gratitude, and keep moving forward.

- Together we are better.

And it vividly illustrates the power of our 5-Step Productive Environment Process™. If you are procrastinating or feeling overwhelmed about a project, take a look at these steps.

1. State your vision.

2. Identify your obstacles.

3. Commit your resources.

4. Design and execute your plan.

5. Sustain your success.

If you haven't started your project yet, focus on the first three steps. Everything you think, say, or feel about the project fits in one of those three steps.

The clearer your vision, the more likely your success. As it says in Proverbs 29:18 (KJV), *"Where there is no vision, the people perish."* However, keep in mind, your vision may, and in my experience, quite likely will, change, but don't give up.

As we often say, "Progress starts with the truth," so write down every obstacle you can think of. You can't change what you don't measure—and writing it down is a form of measuring. New obstacles will arise as you work, but that's normal.

You undoubtedly have resources you haven't thought of, haven't acknowledged, or haven't asked. James 4:2 (KJV) says, *"...ye have not because ye ask not,"* which refers to asking God. That's always a good idea, but it also applies to asking others who not only might be able to help but quite likely would be happy to do so.

Once you have completed the first three steps, you can begin Step 4: Design and execute your plan. To use a phrase my daddy often used on the farm where I grew up, "This is where the rubber meets the road." When you get "stuck," jump to Step 5: Sustain your success. That means going back to Steps 1, 2, and 3 to see what you need to add—or take out—to succeed and change your plan accordingly.

As a follower of Jesus, I believe Romans 8:28 (KJV): *"And we know that all things work together for good to them that love God, to them who are called according to his purpose."* Or, to put it in a Barbara-ism, "It will all turn out in the end. Otherwise, it isn't the end yet."

Blessings,

Barbara

Barbara Hemphill, Founder
Productive Environment Institute
Helping Professionals Accomplish Their Work and Enjoy Their Lives!

CONCLUSION

I am so excited about sharing this book. I wrote my other books because I felt I needed to write them for the sake of our business, but I have written this book for the sake of my heart.

In March of 2020, because of a comment on my social media that reads, "As a follower of Jesus, I pray that other people will feel His love through me, whether or not I ever speak his name, a man from India named Canary contacted me. Of course, as you can imagine, I get many requests from scammers, but my heart told me that Canary's heart was pure, and we began to communicate. He described himself as "Woodcutter, poor wage laborer, teacher for needy children & water carrier for very old people." We communicated virtually every day, but several weeks passed before he disclosed to me that he and his family were digging roots, boiling them, and drinking water to keep from feeling hungry. Because of Covid lockdown, there was no way my husband and I could get any money to him. Of course, my friends and family were extremely concerned that I would consider doing that. Still, I felt compelled for two reasons: I lived in India for nearly five years in the '70s, so I've seen the need, and we adopted three orphans from India who are now amazing adults living in the US, and I know how God can change people's lives when we are willing to help.

One of the first things about Canary that astounded me was his ability to speak and write English because he shared with me that he had only two years of formal education. When I asked him how he had learned, he replied, "My grandfather told me that if I ever wanted to amount to anything, I needed to learn English, so I taught myself!"

Early in our conversation, Canary shared that he felt called by God to be a pastor to share the love of God, but he needed training. In searching for a resource, God led me to Global Hope India, a ministry in North Carolina that offers ministry training and business development to pastors to support themselves and their churches. We have been able to ship Bibles to Canary and his family to begin his ministry through them!

For several weeks, I could not find a way to get money to Canary to buy food and supplies, but Canary assured me that just communicating with him and his family made their life better. One day, my weather app told me their temperature was 55 degrees. When I asked him if they had enough blankets, he responded, "Mom, to tell you the truth, we have only two blankets for five people." (In his culture, it is a sign of respect to call me "mom," -- and his sons call me "Granny." which warms my heart beyond my ability to explain!) On another day, when I saw it was raining, he said, "Somila is happy for the rain because it gives her water to wash clothes." I could write a book -- and one day I will -- about everything I have learned -- and continue to learn -- from Canary and his family. Their tenacity amid struggles that we cannot even begin to imagine continually astound me. Their willingness to share whatever food they have, even when they don't know whether there will be more tomorrow, encourages me to keep giving regardless of the sacrifice.

While living in America is stressful, our lives are luxurious compared to most people in the world. I can't help them all, but I can help one, and I hope you join me. We have embarked on a project we call Shepherd's House Ministry, a home for Canary, his wife Somila, and their four sons Matthew, Mark, Baruch, and Samuel, as well as the people God asks them to help. In addition, it will serve as a center to teach entrepreneurship to the community and, most importantly, share the Gospel of Jesus Christ!

My license plate says HOPEFOOL. When people ask me, "Why?" I reply, "Because I am a fool for Jesus and bringing His Kingdom to this earth, and HOPE stands for Help Others Pursue Entrepreneurship, which has been my passion for over 40 years." Will you please help? Please don't feel ashamed if you can only make a small gift. Remember the loaves and fishes? God's in the business of multiplication.

ABOUT BARBARA

Barbara Hemphill is the **Vision Accelerator.** She works with leaders worldwide who want to ensure that they let God work with and through them to create healthier cultures, more productive workplaces, and a more compassionate world. She helps them clarify and realize their vision for the future. Barbara was chosen in 2022 for Women to Know in America.

Barbara started her career in the organizing industry in 1978 with a $7 ad in a New York City newspaper. Over the decades, she has developed world-class expertise in helping individuals and organizations to tame the chaos and clutter that keep them from being effective, calm, and ultimately free. Her first best-selling book, *Taming the Paper Tiger*, helped her launch and grow the organizing industry.

Barbara founded the Productive Environment Institute in 2008 and has since taught hundreds of Certified Productive Environment Specialists™ worldwide who have helped thousands of people clear clutter, get organized, and ultimately have a better quality of life. Their passion is helping people accomplish their work, enjoy their lives, and help organizations increase profit, productivity, and peace of mind.

Married for thirty-five years, Barbara has three adopted children from India, two stepchildren, and four grandchildren.

In 2020 she launched another passion project—The Shepherd's House Ministry in India—to demonstrate the power of Biblical principles to save lives and foster entrepreneurship. The legacy she invites everyone to share with her is one of creating hope where there is none so that people can live the life God intended for us to enjoy.

To find out more about Barbara, or to book her to speak, go to: https://www.productiveenvironment.com

DO YOU HAVE A PASSION FOR PRODUCTIVITY AND HELPING OTHERS GET ORGANIZED?

DISCOVER HOW TO BECOME AN EXPERT PRODUCTIVITY CONSULTANT IN 90 DAYS OR LESS

www.BecomeASpecialist.com

PRODUCTIVE ENVIRONMENT NETWORK™

EVENTS   ARTICLES   PROGRAMS

LEARN WITH THE EXPERTS
JOIN FREE!

www.ProductiveEnvironmentNetwork.com

The **Shepherd's House Ministry** is a project in Northeast India **prompted by God** and initiated by **Barbara Hemphill** through **Global Hope India.**

Its purpose is to be a home, entrepreneurial development center, and gathering place for sharing the Gospel of Jesus Christ.

"For every house is built by someone, but the builder of all things is God." Hebrews 3:4 (ESV)

WE INVITE YOU TO

GIVE & CONNECT!

 **www.givesendgo.com/shepherdshouse**

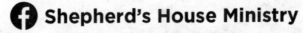 **Shepherd's House Ministry**